All That We See, Say,

Written by
Beth Intro

Illustrated by
Robin Skolsky

Library of Congress Control Number: 2006904652

AuthorHouse™
1663 Liberty Drive, Suite 200
Bloomington, IN 47403
www.authorhouse.com
Phone: 1-800-839-8640

AuthorHouse™ UK Ltd.
500 Avebury Boulevard
Central Milton Keynes, MK9 2BE
www.authorhouse.co.uk
Phone: 08001974150

© 2006 Beth Intro Illustrated by: Robin Skolsky. All rights reserved.

No part of this book may be reproduced, stored in a retrieval system, or transmitted by any means without the written permission of the author.

First published by AuthorHouse 8/8/2006

ISBN: 1-4259-3604-0 (sc)

Printed in the United States of America
Bloomington, Indiana

This book is printed on acid-free paper.

Bloomington, IN Milton Keynes, UK

This, our first book, is dedicated to:

The sweetest memories of seeing my wonderful dad with his beautiful
grandchildren: Annie, Jolie, Zachary, and Seth ---B.I.

Brooke, Marley, and Lindsay's Bubbe, who always
gave us blue skies and sunshine ---R.S.

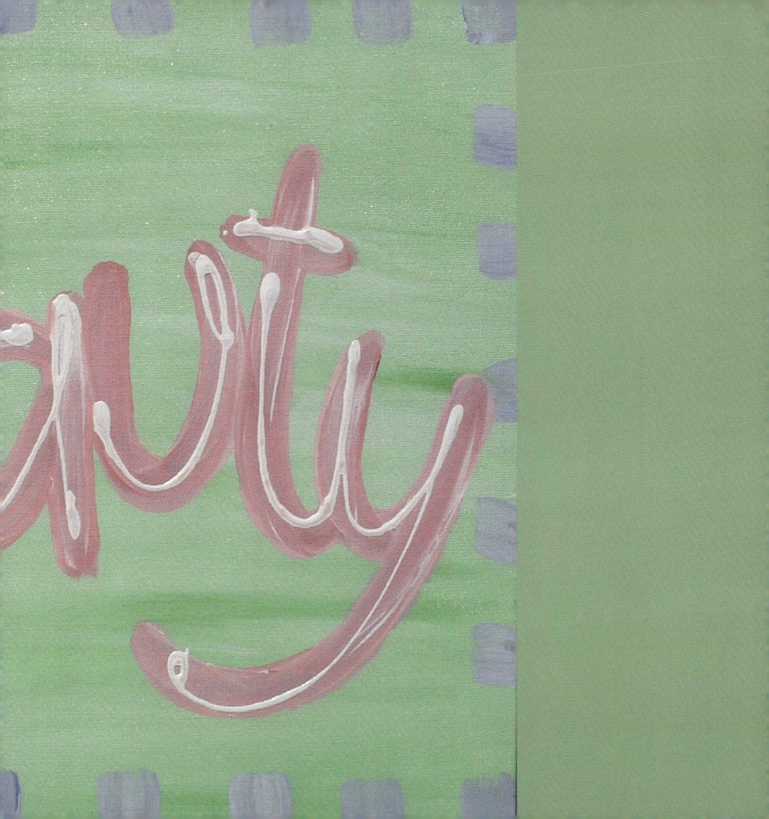

Hashem is in me.
Hashem is in you.
Hashem is in all that we see, say, and do.

Hashem can be seen in
the beauty of trees,
Moving in rhythm to a warm
summer's breeze.

The flowers, the bugs, and
the bluest of skies,
The beautiful grass filled
with striped butterflies.

Hashem is in me.
Hashem is in you.
Hashem is in all that we see, say, and do.
Swish, sway, swee,
Jump, flutter, wee!

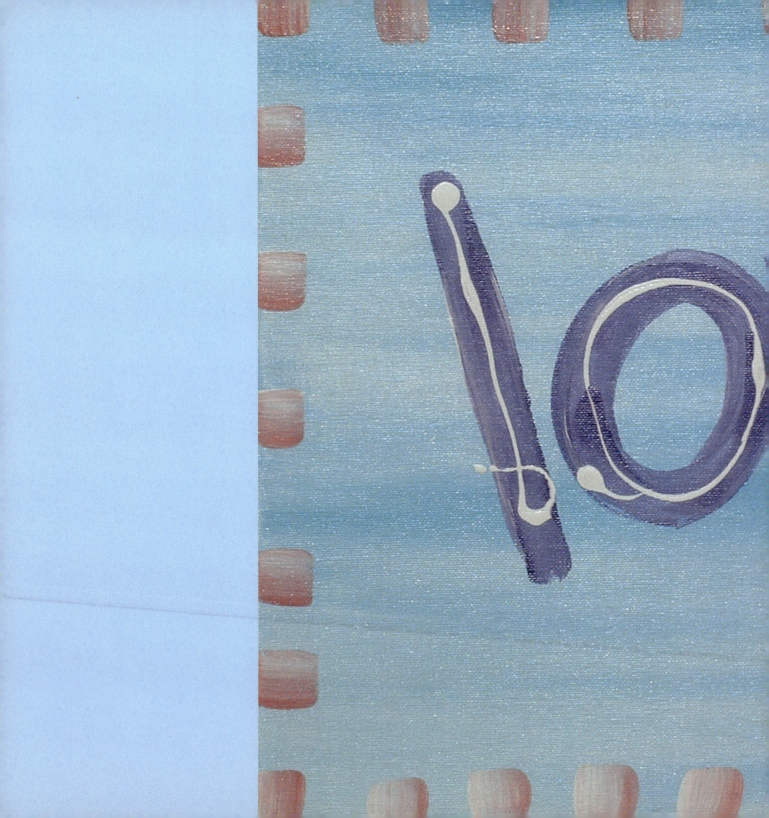

Hashem can be seen in
the love of a mother,
From friend to friend,
from sister to brother.

The love that feels safe when
you know someone cares,
The love that you have to
give and to share.

Hashem is in me.
Hashem is in you.
Hashem is in all that we
see, say, and do.
Kiss, hug, and squeeze me so,
Cuddle, snuggle, and off we go.

Hashem can be seen in the
kindness we show
To the new kid in school and
to people we know.

The kindness that makes
people smile, not fight,
The kindness that comes
with just being polite.

Hashem is in me.
Hashem is in you.
Hashem is in all that we
see, say, and do.
Thanks, excuse me, and pretty please,
Saying bless you for a sneeze.

Hashem can be found looking up, down, and around.
Hashem can be found at the zoo and in the town.
Hashem can be found in the night and in the day.
Hashem can be found at the park where you play.

For when you find BEAUTY and are feeling LOVE so sweet,

For when someone shows KINDNESS to you on your street,

It is Hashem we should THANK for all that we see, say, and do.

Look at me!

I am thankful, too!

About the Author

BETH INTRO, a teacher of young children for over ten years, was inspired to write <u>All That We, See, Say, and Do</u> when her daughter Annie was born. Annie asked endless questions about the colors of flowers and butterfly wings. This is Beth's answer and gift to her children and to children everywhere.

Beth lives in Atlanta, GA with her husband, Craig, and her beautifully curious daughters, Annie and Jolie.

About the Illustrator

ROBIN SKOLSKY, a physical therapist and an artist, has worked with children for many years. Robin works in various mediums including painting on canvas, glass, pottery, and textiles. She especially loves the masterpieces she and her nieces, Brooke, Marley, and Lindsay, create. Robin lives in Decatur, GA. Other examples of her work can be viewed at www.rskolskydesigns.com

Printed in the United States
61457LVS00002B